# How to Make Money off of Other People's Followers

## Ditch the Content Grind and Leverage Other Creators' Audiences

Sapphire Ortega

# Table of Contents

# Introduction

Wouldn't it be nice if you could make money off of followers that aren't even your own? What if I told you that this is the best way to go about things? The approach that most are taking is to try and make money from building their own following, which simply doesn't work and you'll learn why soon enough.

By making money from other people's followers, you can get to the money faster and more consistently. You don't have to wait around for something that may never come.

In this book, you're going to learn why everyone has the wrong idea when it comes to making money on social media, the correct path you need to follow to actually make money in the present age, the different options you have for what you can sell, and how to nurture the leads you create so you can lead them to make a sale. I hope you have an open mind because you won't think the same after reading this.

# Chapter 1: The Old Model Doesn't Work

What's the old way of trying to make money online? Well everyone nowadays wants to be an influencer. We want the validation we get from other people liking the content that we put out there. It makes us feel good.

It makes us feel important. And oh by the way, if you can make money from your followers then why wouldn't you want to do that? If you can get sponsored by a company to promote their product, how could you say no? All you have to do is make a simple post and get paid hundreds or thousands depending on the size of your following.

Who doesn't want to make easy money like that? So you create an account and you get to posting. You post, post, and post some more. And yet there are crickets.

You're barely getting any followers and any likes. You start following your friends and family because you know they'll follow you back and this will be a start at least. Then you start to follow other people in a desperate attempt that they'll follow you back.

You go online and watch videos about how other people built their following. You try to mimic them. You try out the same things they're doing, but nothing seems to click for you.

You're sitting there left scratching your head wondering what you're doing wrong. Why can't you achieve the same level of success that other people have? If they can do it surely you can as well.

## It's Not You

Maybe you've felt like what I've just described to you before and if so I'm sorry. I've been stuck in that same cycle before too and it's miserable. I've sat there wondering why I'm not gaining the following that I'm deserving of.

I would desperately tell myself that the followers and subscribers would come if I just continued to post. I watched every video I could find on how to build a following. I was so jealous wishing that I could have a following just like some of the people I aspired to be.

Now I know better. Now I know that it wasn't me. Too many people are trapped in this obsession with gaining followers, but there's a better way. Think about it, why do you want followers anyway?

Is this about the money or is this about feeling validated by people you don't even know? If you want to feel validated then I'm sorry I can't help you. If this is about the money, then I'm telling you there's a better approach.

In order for you to be successful with it though you must be able to detach from this obsession you might have with feeling like you have to have a following. That can be hard to detach from, but it is truly so freeing once you do. Just know that there was never anything wrong with you. Your approach was wrong.

The approach you were taking was never going to lead you to success or I should say the chances of you being successful by building a following are miniscule. Think about how many people are producing content that you have to compete with. It's simply too much to be able to consistently stand out and next thing you know you're working another full-time job just to post all day for nothing.

Not only that but who's to say that your posts are going to be seen by the people that are following you in the first place? Look at some accounts with a big following and you'll notice that some of them don't have good engagement. This could be a sign that they bought their followers, or it could mean that the algorithm simply doesn't think their content is worth showing because it's not that engaging.

It's no wonder people struggle to find success with this, and yet everyone is still trying to do it so something has to give. The thing that has to give is the craving for followers and instead, become obsessed with building an actual business.

# Chapter 2: The Method

So if building a following isn't the way to go, then what is? Well if building your own following is such a pain and it may never happen, why not go to where the followers are already? If someone else has already put in the effort to build a big following, why not just take advantage of that?

The idea of this might sound crazy but it isn't at all and people have been doing this for decades as a matter of fact. Think about when you watch a television show. You're watching the show and then an ad comes on.

The company is paying the network provider for that ad and the amount they're paying is based on the ratings for the show. So the bigger the audience, the bigger the cost is going to be. Therefore, it's the job of the network provider to play the best shows at the best times to try and maximize profits.

This is why you don't see a sports game playing at 2 am. Sure people might be interested in watching, but not at that time. This is also why shows get canceled.

If it's not bringing in enough eyeballs, then it doesn't matter and it has to go. So essentially the network provider is supplying the people or the "followers" you could say, and advertisers are then paying to be put in front of the "followers." The same premise applies to social media.

You can pay to be put directly in front of someone else's audience. By running an ad, you get to shorten the process of trying to build an audience from scratch before you're able to make any sales. Instead, you can jump to the front of the line.

## Why is This Better?

The reason this is better is because building a brand sounds good in theory, but in reality, it doesn't work. It takes too much time and too much money. Way more money than most people have in fact.

What are the benefits of having a brand? Well, people automatically recognize who you are. There is an inherent amount of trust that people have to know they're not going to get ripped off and that they can request a refund.

So I can understand the appeal of wanting to build a brand. But how many brands do you know of? I'm sure there are quite a few that are coming to your mind right now.

Think about how much money each of those companies are worth. Ask yourself if you can produce even 1/100th of what they do to try and build a loyal following. You simply can't do it, and the good news is that you don't have to.

When you run ads in the right manner, you're able to skip past all of this. You don't have to build a brand or a following. The way that you do this is by being strategic of course.

If you're selling electronics, you run ads on tech channels for example. You don't just throw an ad out there and hope for the best. Even if you're sitting here right now and saying, this is stupid ads don't work!

Well, I would have to disagree with you. Why are we bombarded with ads every day if advertising doesn't work? It does work and you might as well get on the boat.

Everyday people see ads from companies they've never heard of before and they buy because of the ad. Think about how wild that is for a second.

An ad can make someone who wouldn't have known you existed otherwise and turn them into a paying customer.

That is truly wild. The best part is that we don't have to be dealing with radio or TV ads. Those can certainly be effective, but thanks to social media we now have some different options at our disposal.

## Pay Influencers

One option you have is to run ads on social media, but you have another option as well. In the modern age, we have influencers. You don't need to become an influencer to make money.

Instead, you can leverage their following and make more money off of them than what they are making. That's right, I'm talking about influencer marketing and when done properly it is highly effective. For starters, companies are willing to pay hundreds or even thousands to be put in front of certain people's audiences.

So we know that this strategy works, but why does it work so well? It's because people look to influencers as role models. People aspire to be like the people they follow.

Companies have been doing this for ages as well. If you see a commercial with a celebrity in it, that company is paying the celebrity to endorse their product. The company does this because people will buy solely because a certain celebrity endorses their product.

With influencers on social media, things are no different. People will buy your product simply because an influencer that they trust and look up to is recommending your product. The job of the influencer is to post regularly and therefore the followers are regularly seeing everything that they put out.

Thanks to things like stories, people know the ins and outs of this person's life. They're not only family with this person, but they're also very trusting of them and that's why influencer marketing can be so effective. It's not all sunshine and rainbows though.

With anything good, people will naturally try to come in and exploit it. There are some pitfalls you're going to want to watch out for when deciding which influencers you want to pay for and which ones you should avoid.

# Automation is Better

Another benefit to influencer marketing and running ads is that the process is largely automated for you. There's a lot less work that you have to keep up with in order to make money. If you had the choice between automation and manually doing something, which would you choose?

Would you rather use an ice block to keep your food cool or a fridge that keeps your food cool all the time without the need to replace the ice every few days? Do you prefer direct deposit or cashing a check every time you get paid? We like to have automation in our lives and with ads and influencers, you come up with the post and it gets blasted to a lot of people.

This is far better than creating an organic post and having a few people see it, creating another post and a few more people see it, and on and on it goes. Once everything is set up, the money can start to pour in with little upkeep on your part.

# What if You Don't Have Money to Initially Invest?

All of what I've said so far isn't to say that there aren't downsides to what I'm mentioning. The biggest flaw of these methods is going to be money. What if you don't have any extra money to spend on ads?

Well, you're going to need to employ some methods you can utilize that will still be effective but won't cost you any money. As I've talked about before, posting endlessly on social media isn't the best strategy and will leave you spinning your wheels. If you don't have any money though, you're going to have to at least post on a semi-regular basis such as 2-3 times per week.

If you don't do this, then when people do come across your profile, it's going to look dead and they're going to be more hesitant to buy whatever it is you're offering. So when it comes to making money on social media without ads, you really have two to three options you can employ that are effective. The first is to run a contest.

By running a contest, you can get people interested in what you have to offer. Even though they may only care because of the prize, you'll still gain a lot of traction from this because of the exposure you're creating. Let's go into a bit more detail about running a contest now:

## How to Efficiently Run a Contest

Before you run a contest, you have to ask yourself, what's the goal of this contest? Do you want to gain more followers from it? Do you want to increase engagement for one of your posts?

Do you want to make money from it? A contest is good for all of these things. Let's say you want to increase your followers.

Then to enter the contest, you say that you have to be a follower to qualify. You can take things a few steps further though. You can say that to be eligible to win, you must follow this account, like the post, and leave a comment down below.

Now you're not only helping to increase your following, but you're helping to create more engagement on the post, which in turn will help more people see the post. But we're not done yet.

You can have people gain additional entries to win the contest by tagging friends.

You can have this cap at a certain point such as one additional entry for every 3 friends you tag until you reach a max of 10 entries. This is how you can make the most of your contest. Now you're getting friends of friends to see the post.

This can really help to create a lot of exposure for your account. The downside to doing this is that you can only do it every so often. You can't continually run a contest or else your audience will become numb to it.

It does work great though as something you do every now and again such as 2-3 times per year. Now let's talk about prizes. What you give away as a prize is really important to help incentivize people to want to enter the contest.

You could do something generic such as a tablet. That will catch people's attention for sure, but again that's going to be an expense and in this scenario, we're trying to save money. Therefore, to keep things as cheap as possible, we need to make the prizes based on something related to what you're selling.

Let's say you're a coach such as an online personal trainer or business consultant. What you can do is offer free coaching for the first-place winner. This way nothing is coming out of your pocket directly.

This is great and all for incentivizing people to enter the contest, but how do you make money from this? It boils down to making the most out of everyone who entered the contest. What you can do is offer a special discount for anyone who entered the contest and pitch it to every person who entered the contest.

You could do this by making a post about it, but that wouldn't be effective. Everyone who entered your contest likely wouldn't even see the post about the special discount. Additionally, it would be easy for people to ignore and move on.

What is more effective is to directly message each person who entered the contest and directly tell them about the offer. If someone entered the contest because they wanted the possibility of winning free coaching, then they should be interested in receiving the same thing at a discounted rate. This is how you make money from a contest.

You set it up to where it will create a lot of buzz, and then you come in and sell people who entered the contest because the majority of them won't win the contest so it gives you the perfect opportunity to sell them. You want to offer a discount of some sort because this aligns well with the contest. You can say, "Hey you entered the contest and didn't win, but I still want to give you a limited-time offer for entering."

If you offer your product or service at your normal price, then it doesn't feel like the person is getting anything special for entering the contest. The other way that you can have people enter the contest is by DMing you a response. So for instance, you could say I'm giving away 12 free weeks of coaching and to win you have to send me a DM stating why you believe you deserve to win.

If you approach things in this manner, you will get fewer people participating in the contest, but the quality of the leads you're generating will be higher. The people who do enter the contest are going to be far more engaged with the contest and it makes for a much easier time to message them back to continue the conversation and try to convert them into customers.

So for instance, most of the people who send you a DM aren't going to win the contest, but now they've already started the conversation, which makes it easy to continue moving forward from there. You can say something along the lines of,

"Your response was really fire unfortunately there was someone else whose response was just a bit more fire. However, I still want to offer you an exclusive 30% discount on 12 weeks of coaching because your response was amazing. Is that something you would be interested in?"

There are a couple of key elements to this. The first is something I've already talked about, which is the discount. Secondly though, what you're doing is making the person feel special, seen, and heard.

They gave a really good response and they were close to winning, it just wasn't quite there. This is what can really help to push someone to go ahead and buy because you the business owner yourself are telling the person that they did a good job. If you want to make your contest even more personal, then you can have people submit a video for a response to enter.

Have people keep the video to under one minute in length, so you're not spending all day listening to videos. Then when you go to respond to each person, send a video response back to really build that connection. With a video, people will get to hear your tone and see your enthusiasm and this can go a long way in converting sales.

Of course, making people send a video response will decrease the number of participants as some aren't comfortable with making a video. Again though, the quality of each participant will be higher. If you're worried about not getting enough engagement, you can have people enter by either sending a message or video, and then you respond to each person with a video.

This way you'll still be able to add in that personal touch with every person that entered. The cool thing about a contest is that you can do this with physical products, a service, or a digital information product. Later on, I'll be sharing the pros and cons of each type of product or service that you could sell, so don't worry if you're not even sure what you want to do to make money.

If you're selling a physical product, then you will have to give away a product for free, which will cost you money. Then you'll offer other participants a discount. You'll just have to be wary of the discount you offer as you don't want to eat into your profit margins too much.

## How Else Can You Make Money Online Without the Use of Paid Ads or Influencer Marketing?

The second way you can realistically make money on social media organically is by DMing people. That's right, you can message people directly and try to guide people into buying from you. This is no different than going door-to-door or cold calling.

This just has a modern twist to it, which is essentially cold DMing. The difference between cold DMing and cold calling or going door-to-door is that the person can go and scope out your profile. This can help to build trust or be a turn-off depending on what your profile looks like.

This gives you an advantage though compared to cold calling because the person has nothing to go off of. They're just trying to get off the phone and it's hard to trust what the person is saying. Meanwhile, with cold DMing, someone can go to your profile see what you're all about, and see your testimonials to help build trust.

Now when it comes to DMing, you have one of two different approaches. You can message people and try and get the sale off of the first conversation, or you can use the first conversation to build rapport and leave it at that. Then at a later time, you'll come back in the DMs and try to sell them or you'll sell them once they respond to a call to action or something along those lines.

Which approach should you take? Well building rapport will take more time to get the sale, but you'll be far more likely to get it. Think about it.

When someone approaches your door wearing a polo with a company logo and they're holding a tablet, you know you're about to be sold something. They don't care about you, they just want your money. Same thing when you receive an annoying spam call.

So if you and I get annoyed when people try to instantly go for the kill, why would we do the same thing to other people? It doesn't make any sense. Instead, you can be a breath of fresh air to people.

They'll be expecting you to go into a pitch, but it will never happen. They'll start to trust you more, give you a follow, and they'll keep up with what you're doing. You can continue to build rapport with them until the opportunity presents itself to strike.

At this point, they're no longer a cold prospect. They're very warm and the sale will be much easier to make.

## How Do You DM Someone to Build Rapport?

You might be thinking okay this sounds good and all, but why would anyone respond to me in the first place? That's a good point, but you have to remember that people are all about themselves. Therefore, if you come in and start the conversation with something they care about, your chances of getting a response back will dramatically improve.

So look at their profile, and send a message with something unique to them. Maybe they have a post about a video game they're currently playing. You could send a message saying, "Hey how have you liked blank game so far? I was thinking about getting that one myself."

Or maybe they posted about a sports game they went to or some other type of sports-related content. You could send something such as the following: "What do you think about blank's season so far?" The most effective way to go about this is to reply to someone's story.

This way you know they've been recently active and they'll be more likely to respond to what you said about their story. If they don't have anything on their story you can talk about, then finding some content on their feed you can talk about will suffice as well. Once you send the initial message, all you're looking to do is keep the conversation going and continue to talk about whatever it is the conversation started from.

Then once things start to fizzle out you can just let things simmer down just like you would if you were texting a friend. That's honestly how you want to view these conversations. These aren't sales pitches or anything like that.

Talk to people like you would talk to a friend. At the end of the conversation if they haven't already followed you, go ahead and follow them. This will make it more likely that they'll follow you in return.

Now they'll start to see your posts and keep up with you. Over time the relationship will continue to grow and you can then approach them later once they've started liking more of your posts and watching your stories.

Or you can wait until they respond to one of your call to actions, which I'm about to go more in-depth on right now.

## Use Call to Actions

The last way to make money on social media organically is by using a call to action. This is where you make a feed post or story post and you directly call out an action that you want your followers to take.

So for instance, let's say you were making a post about a practical tip that would help your followers increase their productivity. Your post might be something like the following:

"One thing that's helped me be consistent over the years is going to bed on time. The problem with that in the modern age is that there are so many distractions. Sure we might have good intentions every night but then our phones or the TV gets in the way every night. What I did to overcome this is I would set an alarm telling me to start getting ready for bed. This alarm has helped out way more than my regular alarm telling me when to wake up. When my nighttime alarm goes off, I stop what I'm doing and I start my bedtime routine. It helps to "wake me up" from whatever activity I'm getting lost in which is usually my phone. This tip alone has helped me grow my business exponentially."

What I just shared with you is an example of a post without a call to action. This is totally fine as you don't want every single post you make to have a call to action. If you did this, then your audience would start to get burnt out.

What would be worse than doing a call to action every time would be to never do a call to action. So if we took this same post for example and added a call to action to it, now we can make it far more likely that we'll generate sales from it. With call to actions, you want to include them at the end of your post.

This way your audience will have gained value from your post first before you come in with an ask. So in this example, you might say something as follows:

"If you're looking to grow your business with more ninja tips like this, I have 2 consultation spots open right now. If this is something you're interested in, send me a DM with the word "consultation" and I'll send you all the details."

With any call to action you do, there are some key elements that you'll be sure you want to employ to make things more effective. This first thing is relevancy. I'm tying in the call to action with the post I'm making.

I mentioned a helpful trick and in the call to action I'm saying "If you want to learn more ninja tips." The second key element to a successful call to action is urgency. Notice how I said I have two spots left.

This is very important. You want to do something to help create scarcity with your call to action. If you don't do this, then it's easy enough for people to tell themselves they'll get to it later, which of course they never will.

You don't have to create urgency by telling people the number of slots you have available. You could say I'm having a discount but it's only for the first two people that sign up. I'm having a discount but it's ending at midnight.

There are various ways that you can create urgency so don't be afraid to get creative with it. The last key element to this call to action has to do with specificity. It may sound trivial but telling people exactly what you want them to do is important.

In this case, you're telling people to send you a DM containing the word consultation. This takes all of the guesswork out of the equation for the person seeing your post. All they have to do is send the word consultation and they're good to go.

If you don't do something like this, then people will get overwhelmed and overthink things and not reach out to you at all. They'll wonder what they should send to you, how they should reply, and they'll freeze up and send nothing because they don't know what to say. This sounds silly I'm sure, but it's true.

Your call to action won't be as effective if you don't be very hand holdy with what you want people to do. Since we've covered things you do want to do, I want to cover one more thing you shouldn't do. Another mistake people make when doing call to actions is they'll give people two options. Their call to action might say something like:

"If you want to learn more, then click on the link below or send me a message."

When you do something like this people will be confused as to what they should do and they'll end up doing nothing. Again, it seems silly but you don't want to take any chances when it comes to your call to action. In this example, there are way too many assumptions going on.

You're assuming people will know what they should DM you. You're assuming that people who click on the link will know what to do next once they get there, and you're assuming people will be able to choose between the two actions.

Hopefully, you can see why this sets you up for a disaster scenario where your call to action will fall flat on its face. The less you assume with your audience and the more you specify, the better off your call to actions will be.

## So How Many Call to Actions Should You Do?

If a call to action with every post you make is too much then how many should you be doing? Well, it all boils down to the amount that you're posting. If I said one call to action per week is good, but you're only posting once per week, then you're still doing a call to action with every post you make.

So really you should do a call to action every 5 posts or so that you make. If you're posting 5 times per week this will come out to once per week. If you're posting once per day, then you're going to be doing a CTA a little bit more than once per week.

By doing things in this manner, you're ensuring that you're posting enough content in between your call to actions to prevent things from getting stale. You don't want to make it seem like all you care about is making sales.

You want to provide value without expecting anything in return the majority of the time to help build a relationship with your audience. Then every now and again you want to throw something out there so people who are interested can raise their hand.

# Chapter 3: What Are You Going to Sell?

Now that we have the overall foundation laid for how you can generate leads, you first need to decide on how it is you want to make money. There are plenty of different options available to you and each comes with its own set of pros and cons. So let's go ahead and break down some of these things now:

## Digital Information Products

People who sell digital info products can sell them in a video or PDF format, and information products can be found in a wide variety of niches small and big. You have things like business development, fitness, sewing, organization, craft building, fertility, the list goes on and on. There is no shortage of the type of information product that you could create.

Whatever you have in mind, there is probably a market for it. If you create your product in video format, your course will guide people through a topic and each video will be formatted similarly to that of a PDF. You'll have your main intro video discussing a section you're about to dive into and then each video under that section will pertain to that specific subject.

For instance, let's say you're creating a video course about weight loss. One section could be titled What to Eat. You'd have your short 1-minute intro to the section.

Then you could have 3 main videos in the section where you talk about what to eat for breakfast, lunch, and dinner. Then you might have the next section be titled supplements. Then each video in this section would talk about different weight loss supplements someone could take that would be effective.

You would continue this format until the entire course is complete. If your course is in a PDF format, then you would essentially be doing the same thing only it would be broken up into different PDFs. So you'd have a PDF that is solely about the subject of supplements.

Then you'd have a PDF that's all about what meals to eat etc. You want to bust up your different sections into separate PDFs because it makes it appear as if the customer is getting more value as opposed to if all of the information was crammed into one PDF.

Lastly, you could offer a hybrid approach where you have a video course with PDFs supplemented in. So if you had a video where you talked about what to eat for breakfast, lunch, and dinner, you could then create a supplemental PDF that contains all of the meals talked about in the document.

## How Much Should You Charge for a Digital Information Product?

There is a wide range of variance when it comes to pricing with products like this. You could see prices as low as $7 and upwards of $997+. It all depends on the subject.

Usually, digital info products like this will be sold for between $47-$97. The idea is to have a lower price point and then sell at a higher volume. If a product is being sold for $7, then this is typically what's known as a trip wire.

It's meant to provide a lot of value at a low price to essentially try and break the ice with someone spending their first dollar with you. Once the ice is broken, then they'll be more likely to spend more money with you in the future. In terms of core products, typically business to business offerings will be on the higher end of the scale that I mentioned earlier, but that's not always the case.

You might see a business-to-business offering for under $100, but these are the type of products that could sell for $500-$1,000. Something that's business to consumer such as a fitness information product will typically sell for less than $100.

## What Are the Advantages of Selling Information-Based Products

The biggest pro to selling information products is that it can be a very passive way to make money. Once you have your product set up and set to deliver when someone pays you, you really don't have to do much. This is unlike coaching for example, where once you gain a client, the work begins because now you have to serve that client.

You could run an ad, the person goes from your ad to a sales page, and then they buy your product and you don't have to do anything aside from the setup. This in and of itself makes digital info products an intriguing idea to look into.

The other main benefit is that by selling your products at a cheaper price, the entry to make a sale is easier. This isn't to say that it's the perfect way to go about making money though as you'll soon see.

## What Are Some Disadvantages to Information-Based Products

The problem with selling these items at a low price is the sheer amount of volume that you have to sell in order to make a decent amount of money. If you're selling your product in the $500-$1,000 range then of course this is a different story. Let's say though that you're selling a product for $47.

This means you would have to sell roughly 106 copies just to gross $5,000. This doesn't take into consideration your advertising costs or any other expenses you incur. So to make a good chunk of money from this, you're going to have to spend quite a bit on ads to ensure that enough people are seeing your offer.

This is what can make it so tough to truly make money from a low-ticket offer. Essentially, your cost to acquire a new customer is going to be similar to what you're charging for your product in the first place. Therefore, the way that you make money from charging such a low amount is from the lifetime value of a customer.

This is how much money you'll make on average over the lifespan of someone being a customer. Essentially this means you have to sell more and more products to your customer base to ensure that you're able to make money.

## High Ticket Coaching or Service Based Online Business

With this type of product, essentially you are selling a service. With a service, you can make more money because you are doing something for the client rather than just offering information. This is typically done in the form of coaching or consulting.

But it can be done in other ways such as a marketing or ad agency that will actually run ads or make posts on behalf of their clients. Typically, when it comes to a service like this, there's going to be an information piece involved similar to that of an information-based product. This oftentimes means that video courses and PDFs are included as part of the package.

In addition to video courses and PDFs, one-on-one or group coaching will be offered to help people achieve their goals. So for instance, instead of selling an information-based fitness product, you would instead, include that same info product and add to it group coaching or one-on-one coaching.

You could have different offers to help accommodate different level budgets. The highest tier would be one-on-one coaching. The middle tier would be group coaching, and the lowest tier could be just the information.

## How Much Can You Charge for a Service-Based Business

When it comes to pricing, this is where things can get interesting. If you're selling a business-to-consumer type of offer such as fitness coaching, this could range anywhere from $250 per month on the low end up to $1,000 per month per client on the higher side of things. If you're doing business-to-business coaching where you help someone grow a business, things can drastically change and you could be charging up to $3,000 per month or more for one-on-one coaching.

Really the sky is the limit when it comes to business consulting, but this is a very realistic example. If you were managing a big ad spend for a client, it wouldn't be unreasonable to charge $10,000 per month for one client just because the job would be that big!

## What Are the Pros to Running a Service-Based Business?

Right off the bat, it's easy to see that one of the biggest pros to running a consulting type of business has to do with the amount of money that you can make per customer. Back to our fitness example, you'd have to sell 5 courses at $50 a piece to make the same money from selling just one client. That in and of itself is huge.

It is definitely easier to make more from fewer people than to have to acquire more customers to make the same amount of money. Therefore you can make larger amounts of money in a quicker time period when compared to selling information-based products.

## What Are the Cons of a Service-Based Business

For starters, one drawback to a service-based business is the fact that it is more of an active type of income. You're going to have to put in work to acquire clients and continue to put in work to serve them. How you go about selling clients can also change slightly as well.

Instead of an ad leading to a sales page and then converting from there, the process will need to be different. It's a lot harder to sell someone on something that costs thousands of dollars from a sales page. Instead, the process must be more intricate.

This will usually involve messaging someone one-on-one to learn more about their specific situation and then selling them in the DMs or moving the conversation to a phone call where you will then sell them.

# Physical Products

Physical products are everywhere and it's easy to see why you can make money selling a physical product because humans love to buy and acquire things. When it comes to pricing for physical products, this can vary more than anything else I've discussed so far. There are tons and tons of physical products in existence today, so it's easy to see why prices can range so dramatically.

For the purposes of selling physical products online, you're typically going to be selling products that will cost less than $100. Usually, the way this will work is you'll buy your products in bulk and resell them at a higher price. In some cases, you can do what's known as dropshipping where you don't hold any inventory.

Instead, when a customer purchases from you, you then purchase the item from another company, and that company will ship the product directly to the customer. Dropping shipping is by far the easiest way to start selling physical products. You don't have to hold any of your own inventory, but that doesn't mean it's a great idea.

Most of the products you're selling will be sold overseas, meaning that if your customer is in the United States, it's going to take about a month for them to receive their product. In today's world of 2-day shipping, that simply isn't going to fly.

Most people will pass on purchasing simply due to the product taking too long to get to them. To succeed with physical products, you have to be willing to store your inventory so that way you can be competitive with shipping times.

## What are the benefits of selling physical products online?

One of the pros to selling physical products is that there is more trust involved when people buy a physical product compared to something digital. With a digital product, it can be a bit nebulous as to what kind of info the product will contain and if it's actually good or not. With a physical product, people will know what they're getting.

Sure some products are worse than advertised, but if you buy a knife sharpener, you know that's what you're going to get. With an information product, you could spend hundreds or thousands for information that wasn't helpful.

Physical products also give you the ability to make a lot of money. This is because you can sell common items that everyone needs so your customer base can be really big.

## What Are the Drawbacks to Selling Physical Products?

One of the biggest drawbacks to physical products has to do with the products themselves being physical. This alone offers additional challenges. Shipping and storage costs and managing inventory are just a few things that you have to consider.

This is a big deal because you're going to incur costs to store your products. If you dropship, then you're at a disadvantage with shipping times.

There are also the costs you're going to incur to purchase the product yourself, which means that the margins you make from a physical product are going to be quite a bit less compared to a digital product or service.

## Which Method of Making Money Should You Go With?

Ultimately, it's up to you to determine what method of making money you want to go with. If you don't have a lot of money to begin with, then I recommend going with a high-ticket coaching or service option. The reason is that you can more quickly and easily make your first $1,000, $5,000, or $10,000 in profit from this method than the others.

Even if you're tight on cash, it doesn't matter. You can employ organic methods such as cold DMing people to help generate leads. You don't have to store any physical products and you don't have to sell multiple low-ticket offers before you make money off of someone.

Ads only help to fuel this business even more and you have more room for error since the margins you're making per customer are much higher. So if you're not sure what to start with, this is a great choice.

If you go the physical product route and buy a bunch of products just to realize you don't want to do it, well now you're still stuck with the inventory. With coaching, that's not going to be a problem, and then you can always add in a low-ticket offer later on if you want.

# Chapter 4: The Execution to Generate Leads

In this chapter, I want to give you some samples so that you can get an idea of what running an ad might look like. Before we get into the finer details, it's first important to understand the mentality you must have to be successful with either influencer marketing or running an ad.

## Pretend Like You're a Scientist

If you're a scientist and you're trying to discover something, what do you do? You run tests and you experiment. It's not like you're going to try something one time and know that you're going to be successful with it right off the bat.

In fact, oftentimes, you're going to try again and again, sometimes never succeeding. You'll collect data along the way and learn from your past experiments. Sometimes you will succeed and either way, there's something to be learned from each test that you run.

When it comes to running an ad, the same premise applies. You have to put on your goggles and pretend like you're running an experiment. Every ad you run isn't going to be a hit, but by testing and retesting you'll get closer and closer to being successful.

You'll gain valuable data and insights from your ads that don't do so well. Eventually, based on your learnings, you'll be able to tweak things enough to run a profitable ad campaign. This is how you succeed with ads. If you're not able to be patient, then nothing else matters.

## What Type of Ad Can You Run Anyway?

When it comes to running an ad, you could run a search engine ad or you could run an ad on social media. With a search engine ad, you're paying for keywords. Whenever someone types that keyword into the search engine, your website will show up as a sponsored link.

The other way is with social media ads, these are done either with a video or picture, and text is attached. Someone will click on your link and be taken to your website.

From there you can collect an email address, take them to a sales page, or do whatever else. For the purposes of this book, I'm going to be talking about the key aspects of running a social media ad.

## What Matters When Running a Social Media Ad?

When it comes to running an ad on social media, there are multiple things you can target that will determine who sees your ad. For starters, you're going to need to set a daily budget. This is the amount of money that you're willing to spend per day on your ad.

This might be $10 a day or $15, it's your choice and do whatever fits within your current means. Now we need to set our targeting. We can help influence who sees our ad based on a variety of factors such as location, gender, interests, and job title.

So let's say you started a coaching business where you teach people how to code who are interested in getting a job in tech. Well since your business is online, there's no sense in limiting your pool of people by setting a location. Same thing with gender, people of any gender will be interested in what you have to offer, so there wouldn't be a need to limit yourself there either.

Now when it comes to interest and job title, this is where there can be some variance. You have to think about what types of things someone might be interested in who would want to learn coding. I would say to target people who are interested in anything related to technology.

This could be computers, IT, software, programming languages, and possibly video games among other things. As I said, this is where a lot of variance can come into play. You're not going to know what you should target and what you shouldn't.

All you can do is run an ad with interests you think will work and then tweak things from there. Once you have your targeting set, you of course need to have the text and any image or video you're going to be using for the ad ready as well before you launch it. So what might a sample ad look like in this case?

"Has learning how to code always been in the back of your mind, but been something you've never quite been able to get around to? Look things were the same way for me. I was too busy between my full-time job and being a father to ever think I could learn this in-demand skill. That's why I developed a system where I was able to teach myself how to code in just 15 minutes a day. Learning how to code can truly change your life in an instant, and it starts by taking that first leap of faith. If you're interested in learning how to code with just 15 minutes of your day, then click the link below."

The next chapter will show you how to guide people along who do click on your ad. For now though, if you've reached this point, go ahead and pat yourself on the back because you just launched your first ad!

## How to Run a Successful Influencer Marketing Campaign

Since we've covered ads, let's now talk about spending money on an influencer. The thing with an influencer is that there are some traps you can potentially fall into that you don't have to worry about with an ad. Before you spend any money, it's important to take your time and do some research to ensure you're not wasting your money.

## How to Know if an Influencer is Worth Your Time?

With how much money there is to be made from being an influencer, you're undoubtedly going to have some bad apples in the bunch. What I mean by this is you're going to have people who are going to try and fake their way into looking like they're a legitimate influencer. If you don't do your due diligence, then you're going to spend money and nothing will come from it.

This can be frustrating, to say the least, and maybe this has happened to you before. If it has, I don't want a bad experience to jade your point of view on using influencers to help grow your business. When done correctly, it can be a powerful tool to help you reach new heights.

So what signs should you be on the lookout for when it comes to influencers? The first one is going to be the number of followers they have. This seems obvious, but it's not the end all be all. Just because someone has more followers than another account, this doesn't mean they're going to be a better fit.

You have to look at the entire puzzle and this is just one piece to it. Once you see how many followers someone has, you now want to look at how many likes and comments someone gets. There's not a hard rule on how many likes you should be getting per x number of followers.

However, you'll be able to tell if something is off. For instance, if an account has one million followers, but all of the posts consistently get less than 100 likes, this is a bad sign. If there aren't a lot of comments, then this again is another reason to steer clear of handing over any money to this influencer.

Even if their posts get a lot of engagement, this doesn't mean you're in the clear. Of course, people will buy followers to try and look more popular than they actually are, but people can buy likes and comments too. This is something you need to watch out for.

When it comes to likes, take a look at the profiles who like the post and see if they are legitimate. Oftentimes they won't even have a profile picture or more than one or two feed posts. It's easy to see that these are fake accounts liking the post.

When it comes to fake comments, these are easy enough to spot. Most of the time, the comments will just be spam with an emoji or "great post" or "such a fire post." It's comical really.

But wait, there's still more you need to look into. You need to see how many posts this person has. The more posts they've made, the longer they've had their account, the better this influencer's account is.

Lastly, be sure to look at how often they do paid promotions. If every post or every other post they make is about a promotion of some sort, then you should steer clear. This means that their account is over-saturated with promotions and their audience will become numb to all of the promotions if they aren't already.

If you come across a profile that passes all of these tests, then you can go ahead and send them a DM to inquire about a paid promotion. Again though, just because someone has more followers, this doesn't mean that it's a slam dunk. The more followers and engagement someone has, the more it's going to cost you to promote your business.

Therefore, you have to find the right balance for you to ensure that you're not breaking the bank. Once you do find someone you'd like to move forward with, all you need to do is send them a DM asking if they do paid promotions and they'll get back to you if they do. From there you can inquire about pricing and then compare that to other influencers.

# Chapter 5: How to Nurture Leads to Get the Sale

Once you run the ad or do a paid promotion via an influencer, you need to be able to guide the leads that you generate into making the sale. The process doesn't end just because someone clicked on your ad. There are multiple different ways that you can go about nurturing your leads to help warm them up to buy.

## Landing Page to Collect an Email Address

The first method is simple enough. In your ad or influencer campaign, you'll offer some type of free giveaway. This usually will be something like a PDF or a video.

If you were in the fitness space, this might be a checklist such as 10 foods you should avoid to lose weight. In order for the person to get the PDF, they have to click on your link where they'll be taken to a landing page. On this landing page, they'll enter their email address to gain access to the file.

Now that you have their email address, you can send them email campaigns on a regular basis to stay in contact with them. The main goal of email marketing is to provide value and then every once in a while promote your product. So you would regularly send helpful fitness tips and information 2-3 times per week.

Then once every 2 or 3 weeks, you send an email that would have a call to action at the bottom of the email to try and get people to buy your course or sign up for coaching. A call to action in an email works in a very similar manner to that of a social media post.

So let's say you sent an email and the main subject is talking about a food that people should eat more of to keep the weight off. At the bottom of the email, you could have a call to action such as the following:

"Do you want to learn about more foods just like this one that you should eat more of to keep the weight off? I'm currently running a special for my email subscribers that will only last for the next 24 hours. Use the code FOOD20 to receive a 20% discount at the checkout."

## Ad Directly to Sales Page or Video Letter

If you're confident in your copywriting abilities, then you can have people go straight from your ad to a sales page to try and get them to buy. This can be difficult to pull off though if you're copywriting skills aren't on point. Taking someone who's cold and getting them to buy right off the bat is hard to do.

It's easier to make the sale if you spend some time trying to warm up people first. For most people, this isn't something that I would recommend doing, but it's still worth mentioning because it is an option you have at your disposal.

## Join Your Free Community

Another option that has started to become more popular in recent years is running an ad as a way to have people join your free community. Typically this will be in the form of a Facebook group. Let's continue with our fitness example, you could entice people to join your free Facebook group and once they join, they'll gain access to your exclusive PDF that they can't get anywhere else.

So why does being part of a group matter so much? Well for starters, everyone is on social media, so this makes for an easy way to keep in regular contact with people. They'll easily be able to see new updates and posts in the group every time they get on the app.

If they have notifications turned on, then this is even better. But the real magic of the group comes into play with your other members. People will be in there asking questions and soon enough other members will start to chime in and answer questions for you.

This is when you know you've really started to build a community. This community makes it super easy for people to be warmed up, and since it's your group, you get to call the shots. If people aren't abiding by your rules, then you can kick them out.

Having a free group makes it easy to share your content and for group members to see your content. Then just like you would with email marketing, you can promote your products and services every so often. Here's an example of how to do that:

"Hey everyone, as you all know I've been teasing the release of my special one-on-one coaching program that I'm going to be releasing this Friday at noon central time. I'm going to be offering an exclusive 25% discount to members in THIS dedicated community, so stay tuned!"

## Ad to Direct Messaging

Another cool thing about ads is that you can connect them to your direct messages. This means that people can see your ad and then send you a response. So for instance, your ad might talk about a free ebook that you're giving away. All people have to do to get it is send you a DM containing the word "ebook."

From here you can start a conversation with someone and help to get to know more about their situation and warm them up to help propel a sale. So in this instance, you would say something like, "I have your PDF right here for you, I just need to ask you a few questions to make sure that it's a good fit first, is that okay?"

Most of the time, they'll say yes and now you can start to ask them more questions about their current situation. So for fitness, you would ask this series of questions:

-What's your goal?
-What would your life look like if you were able to achieve that goal?
-Why is this goal important to you?
-What have you tried in the past to achieve your goal?

All of these questions are aimed at trying to understand someone's situation better. Once you ask the questions be sure to be empathetic with your responses, you want to show the person that you actually care. Then you can send them the ebook over DM and leave the conversation at that after you ensure that they've followed you on social media.

Now you have someone that you can continue to nurture who you've already built a one-on-one connection with. Eventually just like with organic social media call to actions, they'll respond and you can close the sale from there or reach out when the time is right.

Sometimes you'll be able to tell from messaging someone that they need help right now and they're a hot lead. If that's the case, you can go ahead and pitch your coaching or products during your initial messages after they've responded to your ad.

# Conclusion

Most of the ways that people make money in today's world involve some boring desk job. I say that's lame! Why make money from something that's boring and makes you want to pull your hair out when you could instead make money from something exciting that can be done from anywhere?

You don't need someone else telling you what to do or how much you make. You can be successful without having to build your own following as long as you're patient. Even if you don't have a lot of extra cash to run ads with, that's totally not a big deal.

You can still employ smart organic tactics that are 100% free as I've outlined in this book. It's all about being smart with the resources you have available to you.

And sadly most people don't take advantage of how you can leverage other people's followers in the modern economy. So what are you waiting for? There's plenty of money to be made, so go get your slice of the pie!